Fiddle Tune the Violinist

Jigs, reels, and hornpipes for the beginner to build real violin technique and have fun doing it. With piano accompaniment. By Betty M. Barlow.

& Music Sales America

DISTRIBUTED BY

HAL•LEONARD®
CORPORATION
7777 W. BLUEMOUND RD. P.O. BOX 13819 MILWAUKEE, WI 53213

MW01156790

Preface

Jigs, reels and hornpipes are great fun to play; they are even more enjoyable to perform when appropriately bowed and fingered. This collection of favorites has been carefully edited to make it possible for the student and amateur violinist to build real fiddling skills.

The dances have been arranged in order of difficulty and are in the easy "fiddle keys" of G, D and A. Through the practice of these lively folk melodies, the violinist will develop:

Rhythmical playing
Ability to maintain steady tempo
Improved articulation
Speed and precision in finger action
Coordination between the hands
Bowing techniques (accent, staccato, legato, etc.)
Wrist flexibility in string crossings
Endurance
and
Enthusiasm for impromptu performance!

Betty M. Barlow

Cover design by Barbara Hoffman
Cover photograph by Herb Wise

Copyright © 1977 by Amsco Publications,
A Division of Music Sales Corporation, New York, NY.

Order No. AM 40882
International Standard Book Number: 0.8256.2198.4

Exclusive Distributors:
Music Sales Corporation
257 Park Avenue South, New York, NY 10010 USA
Music Sales Limited
8/9 Frith Street, London W1V 5TZ England
Music Sales Pty. Limited
120 Rothschild Street, Rosebery, Sydney, NSW 2018, Australia

Printed in the United States of America by
Vicks Lithograph and Printing Corporation

Contents

White Cockade

Irish Reel

Durham Rangers

Hornpipe

The Rakes of Mallow

Country Dance

Tom and Jerry

Scotch Reel

Turkey in the Straw

American Pioneer Tune

Soldier's Joy

Hornpipe

Reilly's Reel

Traditional

Fagin's Holiday

Jig

Arkansas Traveler

Traditional American Tune

Rustic Dance

Reel

Miss Johnson's Hornpipe

Traditional

The Emerald Isle

Irish Jig

Garry Owen

Jig

The Rose

Irish Reel

The Devil's Dream

Reel

Staten Island

Hornpipe

Irish Washerwoman

Jig

Miss McLeod's Reel

Traditional

Durang's Hornpipe

Traditional

Wind That Shakes the Barley

Reel

Paddy Carey

Jig

Fisher's Hornpipe

Traditional

Paddy Whack

Irish Jig

Nimble Fingers

Reel

Dominion

Reel

Billy the Barber

Irish Jig

Fine

Fine

D.C.

D.C.

Gilderoy

Hornpipe

Flower of Donnybrook

Irish Reel

Vaughan's Favorite

Jig

Liverpool Hornpipe

Traditional

Quindaro

Hornpipe

St. Patrick's Day in the Morning

Irish Jig

Fireman's Reel

Traditional

Huntsman's Hornpipe

Traditional

Delaware

Hornpipe

Go to the Devil and Shake Yourself

Jig

An Old Reel

Irish

The Break Down

Hornpipe

Larry O'Gaff

Irish Jig

New Century

Hornpipe

Cincinnati

Hornpipe

Chandler's Hornpipe

Traditional

46

Hunting the Hare

Jig

Fred Wilson's Hornpipe

Traditional

© 1977 Amsco Music Publishing Company All Rights Reserved.

GREAT FIDDLIN' FOR EVERYONE

English, Welsh, Scottish & Irish Fiddle Tunes
by Robin Williamson
An outstanding collection of the traditional fiddle tunes of Britain. Not intended as a tutor, the book is meant to give someone who can already play a bit insights into the tricks and graces of traditional playing. More than 100 tunes, edited and annotated, which can also be played on mandolin, tenor banjo, flute, accordion, concertina, etc. Guitar chords have been added, and the pieces are arranged from easy to advanced.

O'Neill's Music of Ireland/ Revised
by Miles Krassen
Miles Krassen has gathered and re-edited more than 900 fiddle tunes, bringing up-to-date Capt. Francis O'Neill's famed collection of Irish dance music, jigs, reels, hornpipes, long dances and marches. Included are new settings from the recordings of legendary Irish musicians such as Michael Coleman. All music is re-engraved and a cross-reference title index has been added. Also included are many tips on getting the authentic feel of Irish music.

Bluegrass Fiddle
by Gene Lowinger
A comprehensive guide to playing the fiddle, bluegrass and country style, from Gene Lowinger, who has played with Bill Monroe. With 29 bluegrass and 14 traditional tunes.

Appalachian Fiddle
by Miles Krassen
58 transcriptions of breakdowns, jigs, hornpipes and modal tunes. Includes instructions on traditional fiddle styles, bowing techniques, double stops chart & discography. $3.95